ROCKY MOUNTAIN
NATIONAL PARK

TO BOULDER

7

ROOSEVELT NATIONAL FOREST

Longs Peak Camp

Basin Camp

Chasm Lake

X Meeker Peak

WILD BASIN

Thunder Lake

North St. Vrain Creek

Bluebird Lake

Longs Peak X

Alberta Falls

The Mills Lake
Loch

Bear Lake

X Hallet Peak

Andrews Glacier

Taylor Glacier

CONTINENTAL DIVIDE

Lake Nanita

Lake Verna

PARADISE PARK

Cascade Falls

WEST PORTAL

Grand Lake

GRAND LAKE ENTRANCE

BIG MEADOWS

ARAPAHO NATIONAL FOREST

Grand Lake

Shadow Mountain Lake

Colorado River

North Fork Colorado River

ARAPAHO NATIONAL RECREATIONAL AREA

Lake Granby

34

RANGE

ROCKY MOUNTAIN
NATIONAL PARK
BEYOND TRAIL RIDGE

PHOTOGRAPHY BY WENDY SHATTIL AND BOB ROZINSKI
TEXT BY BUDD TITLOW

WESTCLIFFE PUBLISHERS, INC. ENGLEWOOD, COLORADO

CONTENTS

International Standard Book Number:
ISBN 0-942394-22-4
Library of Congress Catalogue Card Number:
86-050064
Copyright, Photographs: Wendy Shattil and Bob
Rozinski, 1986, 1991. All rights reserved.
Copyright, Text: Budd Titlow, 1986.
Book Designer: Gerald Miller Simpson/Denver
Illustrations: Ann Pappageorge
Maps: Ann W. Douden
Typographer: Edward A. Nies
Printed in Japan by Dai Nippon Printing Company, Ltd.
Tokyo
Published by Westcliffe Publishers, Inc.
2650 South Zuni Street
Englewood, Colorado 80110

*First frontispiece: Indian paintbrush in a subalpine
meadow*

Title Page: The Diamond of Long's Peak at sunrise

Right: Autumn snow on aspen trees below Hallet's Peak

PREFACE

The uniqueness of Rocky Mountain National Park is best experienced by making the effort to look beyond the obvious natural wonders of this preserve, one of America's magnificent resources. Park visitors always enjoy the scenics and wildlife; however, many people miss the true character and excitement found by looking Beyond Trail Ridge.

As we explored the park through the eye of the camera and found such a diversity of images, we became eager to share our discoveries. In this book are sights which can be observed with minimal effort by simply slowing down and taking the time to look. In return you might glimpse a cow elk with her calf browsing the greenery adjacent to Trail Ridge Road or enjoy the impressionistic quality of summer carpets of wildflowers. You might catch the first rays of sunrise spotlighting the Continental Divide, or overlook the fog-blanketed Kawuneeche Valley, or discover the brilliantly colored male bluebird flying with breakfast for his young.

Over the many months of photographing for this book, we kept an extensive journal of observations. Many entries are included as captions accompanying our images. The journal made us aware of the time clock by which all living things function in Rocky. A species of flower blooms and dies and is replaced by another. Growth of vegetation and the needs of wildlife coincide. Insect populations and other food supplies peak when birds most urgently need a constant source from which to feed their young. Tundra vegetation must be harvested by pika and marmots for food or to provide insulation for their burrows through the winter.

In documenting our observations, especially through the short Rocky summer, we saw subtle changes in weather patterns influence the entire park. A great deal of Rocky lies within the world of alpine tundra, where conditions are so harsh virtually every living thing is balanced on the edge of existence. Slightly less than average precip-

itation can change last year's carpets of alpine flowers to this year's comparatively bleak expanse. The summer season at this altitude is compressed and everything lives at an accelerated rate.

The photographs in this book were made with lenses from 20mm to 700mm on 35mm cameras. Virtually any type of camera, from Instamatic to Hasselblad to video, may be used to capture the many wonders of Rocky; but the person behind the camera is the most important thing. Once you acquire the skill of finding the subjects, a camera can transfer onto film an infinite array of timeless images. These will aid in the recollection of personal experiences with wild things in wild places.

Sometimes it's best to put the camera down when visiting Rocky. Concentrating on composing an image and operating a camera can prove a distraction. For the purest enjoyment, leave the camera in the car. Listen for the chatter of the chickaree and the hoot of the great horned owl. Smell the forget-me-nots. Dip your fingers in the icy streams. The richness of Rocky is all around. Simply learn to see it and in turn, respect it.

This book would not be complete without expressing our gratitude to a few of the many people who helped us along the way. Budd Titlow's broad knowledge of the Rockies contributed greatly to our productivity with the camera. He joined us many times to see, experience, and take part in our discoveries. We appreciate David Dworkin's strong back and his assistance carrying equipment to shooting locations. Our pilot, Susan Rhodes, and navigator, Annie Douden, gained us a perspective of Rocky from the air. Thanks go to George and Louise DeLella for offering us a secluded base camp. The support and information extended by the rangers and naturalists of Rocky Mountain National Park were invaluable, and we are especially grateful to the staff of the backcountry office for their efforts.

Wendy Shattil and Bob Rozinski

MALE BLUEBIRD NEAR NEST IN ASPEN TREE. An excellent way to improve your birdwatching is to sit quietly in an aspen grove for an hour or two in late spring. A grove that at first glance seems devoid of activity may actually support many nests. For example, this bluebird, a tree swallow and a flicker were nesting in this same tree.

Overleaf: SUNRISE AT SPRAGUE LAKE. Sunrise in the park offers spectacular views of the rugged alpine landscape. The first light of the sun clearing the horizon is often intense, coloring the cloud-shrouded peaks with pastel hues.

INTRODUCTION

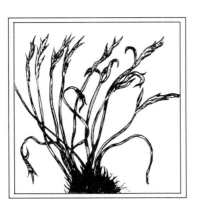

Rocky Mountain National Park is known in the recreation industry as a "drive-through park." Proximity to Front Range population centers and accessibility from several major highways make "Rocky" a must-see for most people vacationing in Colorado. Yet a majority of the park's three million annual visitors don't really get to experience what the park is all about. The average length of stay is only seven hours; long enough to stop at a couple of scenic turnouts, view the magnificent mountain panorama, have lunch and maybe take a short stroll along a tundra interpretive trail. This is unfortunate because there's so much more to see and do here than meets the eye during a quick trip across Trail Ridge Road.

The allure of Rocky is a subtle splendor that can best be seen by those who venture off the asphalt and away from the crowds. It's the pastel fragrance of a bouquet of stream-side columbines; the chattering of a chickaree from high up a lodgepole pine;

the slap of a beaver's tail on a sunset-muted pond. It's all the essential, magical qualities of nature that come together to make Rocky Mountain National Park what it truly is . . . an ecological showcase for the western United States.

No other park offers a better opportunity to see and study the wild plants and animals that make up the various "life zones" found throughout the Rockies. Driving up Trail Ridge Road, a park visitor travels — ecologically speaking — from the open ponderosa pine forests so typical of the Colorado foothills to the treeless tundra characteristic of northern Alaska in a distance of less than ten miles.

Let's examine some of the ecological wonder of Rocky by looking through the eyes of widely-acclaimed nature photographers Bob Rozinski and Wendy Shattil. The photographs that adorn these pages artfully reveal the exquisite natural beauty that lies hidden "Beyond Trail Ridge."

BACKLIT SPIDER WEBS. Many unusual sights can be found when the weather is less than optimal. This phenomenon occurred early one foggy morning near Onahu Creek. Once the sun burned through the clouds, the webs lost their glistening outlines.

CALYPSO ORCHID IN WILD BASIN. Despite its delicate beauty and bright color, this orchid eludes the casual observer. But if you do find one along the trail, your eye suddenly seems to realize what it is looking for and many more appear.

FROST-RIMMED VEGETATION ON SHORE OF POUDRE LAKE. These frost patterns were found on an overcast, misty morning. All the groundcover near the lake was coated with delicate ice crystals that melted when the sun broke through the clouds.

PONDEROSA
WOODLAND

The rolling forests of ponderosa pine which decorate the park's eastern foothills are fountains of breezy delights. These widely-spaced, long-needled pines give rise to a variety of ground cover plants, including patches of glowing grasses and a host of shrubs. Their fragrant orangish-brown plated bark has been described as smelling like everything from vanilla to butterscotch. Because of the range of habitats and relatively mild climate, the ponderosa forest is home to the most diverse bird population in the park.

Ecologists will tell you there's no such thing as a true blue pigment in nature. Watching the mountain bluebird in lilting flight across a sage-choked meadow makes that difficult to believe. The sun's rays glinting off the bird's back produce a richly-luminescent sheen that is unmistakable and irresistible.

Chances are in early July, the bluebird — cheeks crammed full of insects — will be returning to a nest hole in the trunk of a dead or dying ponderosa. The bluebird is mainly a cavity nester, illustrating the need for dead standing timber in the forest ecosystem. If all the dead trees are removed, such cavity-nesting birds would have difficulty reproducing and might soon disappear from an area. For this reason, in Rocky as well as many other natural areas, dead trees are allowed to stand until blown down or toppled by some other means.

The western tanager, with his brilliant red head, yellow body and black wings, is the most strikingly-colored bird in the park. More than a few naturalists have lamented the fact that this is not Colorado's state bird instead of the comparatively dull black and white lark bunting of the eastern plains.

Look closely and you may see the unusual behavior of a tiny, stubby tailed pygmy nuthatch. Descending a ponderosa tree trunk headfirst in a continual assault on insects, he utters a soft "pip-pip-pip."

You'll probably hear the distinctive trilling flight of the broad-tailed hummingbird before you actually see one. This tiny, but bold, nectar lover often molds a lichen-and-cobweb nest on a head-high ponderosa branch. She then sits motionless and all but invisible as she incubates her sparkling-white, pea-sized eggs.

The ponderosa forests are also home to a striking black and white, plank-tailed fellow who seems to delight in outsmarting everything, especially human picnickers, who enter his territory. He's the "thieving magpie" of Shakespearean fame, and a few minutes of watching his pilfering will prove he lives up to his name. If you turn your back for just a few seconds, he'll be there perched beside your plate and ready to whisk half a sandwich away from under

ABERT'S SQUIRREL ON PONDEROSA TRUNK. The long tufts of hair on the ears help identify this elusive tree squirrel. The Abert's coat ranges from light tan to pure black. While these squirrels are common in the park's campgrounds, a keen eye is required to pick them out from perches high in the trees.

Overleaf: FALL RIVER, MEANDERING THROUGH HORSESHOE PARK. This snake-like pattern, produced by sunrise light reflecting off the water's surface, illustrates that flowing water reaching a level area often follows a path of least resistance rather than moving in a straight line.

your nose. If he succeeds at his larceny, which he somehow seems to do with uncanny regularity, he may swoop away with his booty and bury it under a nearby ponderosa before quickly returning for another strike.

Another raucous picnic table hopper frequently seen in the ponderosa woodland is the Steller's jay. With his pompadourish crest and cobalt blue and black plumage accentuated by white facial stripes, this gregarious bird always looks as if he's dressed for a night on the town. The Steller's jay fills the same role, known as a niche, in the ponderosa pine forest as the bluejay does in the deciduous forests of the eastern United States. Such closely related species living in different geographic regions are known as ecological equivalents.

It's a matter of conjecture as to whether food-caching birds, such as the magpie, Steller's jay, and Clark's nutcracker actually remember where they hide their foodstuffs. Some researchers believe they rely on simple hit-or-miss searching techniques; the theory being if enough birds cache enough food there will be plenty for all to find come winter. Whatever technique they use, it works quite well. There always seems to be plenty of magpies and Steller's jays flitting among the ponderosa branches.

As the late afternoon sun lengthens the stolid shadows of ponderosa branches up into the crests of nearby ridges, you may see the western mule deer browsing languidly among the shrubs on the sun-soaked, south-facing hillsides. The mule deer is distinguished from his close cousin, the eastern whitetail deer, by extra large ears and antlers which branch equally, instead of as prongs from a main beam. The mule deer is also the more curious of the two, and when spooked will invariably stop, turn around and sneak a peek at its pursuer. This attribute makes these deer quite vulnerable during hunting season in non-protected areas.

For the mule deer, the ponderosa pine forest is a smorgasbord of tasty delights. The abundant, three-lobed foliage of the bitterbrush is his staple food, the meat-and-potatoes of his diet, while the harder to find, feather-seeded mountain mahogany is the much sought after dessert. For a change of pace and taste, there are the reddish-gray barked squaw-currant, several types of spicy sagebrush and the succulent leaves of shrubby cinquefoil.

Because of the sparse timber and relatively mild winters, ponderosa pine forests are as attractive to humans as they are to wildlife. In fact, if it weren't for the protection of the park, most of the ponderosa woodland surrounding Estes Park would soon be taken over by subdivisions, shopping centers, and other commercial development. One uniquely-adapted animal that would suffer from such an occurrence is the Abert's or tassel-eared squirrel.

If you look carefully, you might be able to pick out the furtive figure of an Abert's squirrel nestled among the uppermost branches of a tall ponderosa. This curiously-silent rodent has tufted, hornish-looking ears and a sheeny coat that ranges from solid black to metallic silver. The Abert's is extremely "habitat specific," meaning that he can live only in the ponderosa pine forests of the park's lower elevations.

As you examine the various ecosystems in the park, keep in mind that not everything has been preserved in absolutely pristine condition. Some portions of Rocky, particularly the ponderosa pine forests, were impacted by the activities of man — grazing, logging, homesteading and mining. Many of these disturbed areas have significantly recovered since Enos Mills, the park's founding father, pushed through legislation in 1915 establishing Rocky Mountain National Park. Yet the scars of human use and misuse, some quite visible and others not so evident, still remain in many places. Since its inception, the park's staff has been attempting, "wherever physically, financially and politically possible," to restore the park's resources to conditions that existed prior to the 1800s.

One of these efforts involves the acquisition of in-holdings, parcels of land within the park's established boundaries that still belong to private individuals. According to the Chief Naturalist, one of the park's management goals is to achieve "100 percent federal ownership" by buying the remaining inholdings. Once this is accomplished, buildings and other signs of human activities would be removed and the land would be allowed to revert to natural conditions.

SUNRISE VIEW FROM RAINBOW CURVE. Early morning haze in the valleys creates the phenomenon known as atmospheric perspective, which leads to the stacking effect and the illusion of distance.

MONTANE
PARKS

On the east side of Rocky, the rolling ponderosa hillsides are interrupted in several places by open, grassy expanses known as montane "parks." These meadow-like areas, such as Horseshoe and Moraine Parks, feature heavy soil deposition and high water tables, a combination that is much more conducive to the growth of grasses and wildflowers than trees and shrubs.

Moraine Park, along the road to Bear Lake, was formed when a glacier gouged a valley here. Its present broad, tabletop-flat configuration resulted when sediments accumulated in a temporary lake on the valley floor. When the glacier melted, in response to a warming climate, it left piles of rock rubble — known as moraines — along each side of Moraine Park.

Standing in Moraine Park, you can see a continuous, heavily-forested ridge to the south. This is one of the finest examples of a side or lateral moraine in the world. There is also a much less discernible end or terminal moraine, left by the toe of the melting glacier, at the eastern end of Moraine Park.

Parks, with their luxuriant assortment of grasses and flowering plants, provide excellent winter grazing habitat for some of Rocky's ungulate or hooved mammals. A predawn visit to Horseshoe Park may be rewarded by the sights of a herd of grazing elk or a group of bighorn rams sauntering down to a salt lick.

If you try to find these animals, please keep in mind that the National Park Service is extremely concerned about harassment of wildlife. They ask that, for the safety of both people and animals, you maintain a safe distance.

A good rule of thumb is to approach no closer than 50 yards, unless the animal shows signs of stress before then. Even a seemingly docile mule deer doe can, when aroused, use her razor-sharp hooves to inflict serious injury.

Also, please respect all restricted areas, such as the "No Stopping Zones" along the Horseshoe Park Road. Bighorn sheep are particularly susceptible to human interference, and even minor disturbances could stress them past their tolerance limits.

Moraine and Horseshoe Parks are also excellent places to spot predatory animals, such as the much maligned coyote and the energetic badger. On nightly hunting forays, the coyote — a bushy-tailed relative of the domestic dog — is a classic example of an omnivore. He'll try to eat just about anything he comes across, from grass to grasshoppers and jackrabbits. Because of this opportunistic palate, the coyote is regularly labeled as a wanton killer of livestock — the rancher's Public Enemy No. 1.

Lost in the throes of this continuing controversy is the coyote's proven ability to keep local rodent populations in check. Without him, we could very well be up to our waists in field mice within just a

WOOD LILY BESIDE CUB LAKE TRAIL. With its size and brilliant color, the wood lily provides an unexpected floral bonus to those visitors hiking the park's lower elevations. These wildflowers are such an attraction that admirers sometimes unknowingly trample vegetation surrounding the blossoms.

few years. Fortunately, because of the coyote's wile, cunning and an uncanny ability to adapt to just about anything humans do to control him, we'll never have to find out what life without him would be like. His frenetic yip-yapping will always be there to add that hauntingly-comfortable quality to moon-lit western nights.

If you really want to have some fun, try and find a badger out on his morning hunting rounds . . . but be sure and stand back! When this stumpy-legged, grayish-yellow member of the weasel family puts his shovel nose and long fore-claws to work, his prey — usually a plump whitetail prairie dog or Richardson's ground squirrel — doesn't have a chance. With dirt flying in all directions, you'll soon under-stand why the badger is considered the king of nature's excavators.

The badger is often mistaken for its cousin the wolverine, a fierce and fearless predator — called the "devil dog" by terrified pioneers — you're not likely to see in Rocky. Along with the grizzly bear and gray wolf, the wolverine was probably extirpated — eliminated — from Colorado's Front Range sev-eral decades ago. The many unfounded myths and legends about these "horrible beasts" made them the subjects of widespread fear and loathing and prime candidates for being shot on sight.

We now understand the value and need for such top carnivores in the ecosystem, insofar as keeping populations of deer and elk under control and maintaining a good overall ecological balance. But for the grizzly, wolf, and wolverine, this understand-ing has come too late. Even if we could accept them back into our crowded mountain communities, the fact is that they are the kindred spirits of the true wilderness and, as such, simply can't abide by the presence of man or his activities.

A common wildflower of montane parks is the paintbrush. This semi-parasitic plant obtains part of its nourishment by attaching to the roots of other plants. The paintbrush's bright colors are contained in modified leaves, known as bracts, instead of flowers. There are several varieties of paintbrush in Rocky, ranging from the flaming red of lower eleva-tions to a pale yellow specimen found on the tundra.

Another familiar floral sign, growing in clusters in the wetter areas of open parklands, is the violet-blue blossom of Rocky Mountain iris. This distinctive plant with narrow, swordlike leaves and slender, erect petals is also know as the "fleur-de-lis" because of its standing as the official emblem of France.

COYOTE IN HORSESHOE PARK. This highly adaptable predator is an integral part of the park's ecosystem. Like many animals within the park, the coyote is most often seen at sunrise or sunset.

Overleaf: BACKLIT ASPEN AND GOLDEN BANNER IN HORSESHOE PARK. An aspen grove is a purely tranquil environment, a feeling accentuated by showing late afternoon light streaming through the branches. This gives a mood totally different from that typically seen during the middle of the day.

DOUGLAS FIR
FOREST

Many of the north-facing slopes in the park's lower elevations are covered with a dense carpet of Douglas fir, a forest type that is the antithesis of the ponderosa pine woodland. Sometimes the spindly-branched fir trees grow together in such a foreboding mass, they block out the sun and severely limit the growth of understory plants. The tightly-compacted, inch-long fir needles can stifle even the slightest breeze, giving the forest a stuffiness that makes just standing still seem uncomfortable.

Looking up into such monotonous forest canopy, you can easily understand why the local wildlife population finds the Douglas fir forest so uninviting. It's like touring a subdivision where every home is exactly alike. Who wants to live in a place with no diversity . . . no character? The saying "variety is the spice of life" applies equally to wildlife and humans. For with wildlife the rationale is survival instead of simply pride and self-esteem.

In nature, diversity is the keynote to maintaining a healthy and productive ecosystem. A monotypic vegetative community yields an equally non-diverse wildlife population. Because of this, about the only thing you can expect to see in a dense stand of Douglas fir is the chickaree — the ubiquitous tree squirrel — chipping away at the unending supply of fir cones.

CLAVARIUS PURPURCEA GROWING ON THE FOREST FLOOR. As shown here, mushrooms are a very diverse group. Many of them don't look anything like the common grocery-store varieties. This purple, coral-like specimen was one of about twenty different mushroom types growing in a small area.

MULE DEER DOE AND NURSING FAWN.   June is the month to watch for newborn mule deer fawns, though their mothers keep them well hidden. For protection, the doe may signal her fawn to drop to the ground and freeze until danger has passed. Because of this, never assume that a fawn curled in the grass is abandoned. In most cases, the mother is watching intently from a nearby hiding place.

TUMBLING CASCADE AND CHIMING BELLS.   These water-loving wildflowers often line the banks of fast-flowing streams in the park. Such streamside or riparian environments often support extremely diverse plant communities.

RIPARIAN
ZONE

Riparian habitat, the vegetation growing along a watercourse, is one of the most valuable, yet fastest-disappearing natural resources in Colorado. For those of us living in this state's semi-arid climate, riparian zones are especially important as ribbons of life-giving moisture coursing through often parched and unyielding terrain. For wildlife, they are nature's drinking fountains and protected passageways for migrating from one habitat type to another. They give root to an amazing diversity of plant life from the towering blue spruce, Colorado's state tree, to amorphous masses of rock-coating algae.

There are primarily two types of streamside riparian habitat in Rocky: snakelike bands of willows that meander through montane parks and high mountain valleys, and lush borders of water-loving plants along fast-flowing mountain streams.

One of the best examples of meandering, willow-choked habitat can be seen beside the Cub Lake Trail winding along the west end of Moraine Park. Here you can find fragrant bouquets of the Colorado blue columbine nestled beside the rushing headwaters of the Big Thompson River.

The columbine, Colorado's state flower, has suffered the indignity of almost being loved out of existence. Around the turn of the century, when trainloads of tourists first began to venture into the Colorado mountains, the columbine was a common sight. So common, in fact, that travellers soon began to regard the large, teacup-shaped blossoms with impunity and regularly dug them up for home landscaping and commercial use. This attitude did not bode well for the perennial columbine which was being robbed of its reproductive root stock each year. In just a few years, the popular blossoms became extremely difficult to find. Luckily the plight of the columbine was noted by a few forsighted legislators. They passed the Columbine Protection Act, which made the plucking of columbine blossoms punishable by fines and jail sentences. This legal deterrent, coupled with peer pressure from enlightened citizens, worked wonders. Within a few summers, the columbine was well on its way to recovery. Now the cream-and-sky-blue blossoms are quite abundant in the park for us all to see and enjoy.

As you walk along the ponderosa-covered hillside, don't be surprised if you suddenly see a pair of round chocolate-brown ears and a cream-colored face pop up from behind a trailside rock, disappear and pop up for another look a few seconds later. This diminutive, elongated creature is the long tailed weasel, also called the ermine when he turns pure white during the winter.

The tepid, lily pad-covered water of Cub Lake provides ideal habitat for the leopard frog and the tiger salamander, two of a handful of cold-blooded animals that can withstand Rocky's frosty climate. In fact, if you've heard any snake stories about the park, you can forget them. The only snake known to occur here is the harmless gray garter snake. There are no rattlers or other poisonous species.

Pure, crystalline stream water can take a variety

PARRY PRIMROSE AND TIMBERLINE FALLS ABOVE THE LOCH. The many backcountry waterfalls scattered throughout the park are a delight to explore. The mist and damp ground surrounding a waterfall produce a unique community of plants that would otherwise not have enough moisture to survive.

Overleaf: CHAOS CASCADES AT FIRST LIGHT. Looking down instead of up, the cascade of a waterfall presents an entirely different perspective. The light of dawn envelopes the landscape in a special glow and gives the water a rich luminescent sparkle.

of routes down the park's rock-laden mountainsides. These range from gently-tumbling Chaos Cascades near Bear Lake to the sheer drop of Timberline Falls just above the Loch.

A hike up to Mills Lake from the Glacier Gorge Trailhead will take you along a prime example of a bouncing, evergreen-sheltered mountain stream. The most amazing resident of such a habitat is a bird that can actually walk, swim and fly under water. The slate-gray, wren-like water ouzel feeds by diving into the frigid water and plucking aquatic insects off the stream bottom. This thrush-sized bird's curious habit of constantly bobbing up and down while perched on streamside rocks has given him the nickname of "the dipper." A pair of ouzels typically builds a mossy, oven-like nest right in the spray of a rocky cascade.

After arriving at Mills Lake, you'll want to prop your feet up on a convenient rock and soak in the magnificent mountain vista. Towering above will be the massif of Longs Peak, the tallest and most famous mountain in the park, and the starkly-sculpted Keyboard of the Winds.

The Yellowstonesque, willow-lined shores of Onahu Creek on the park's west side provide ideal habitat for a toothy, paddle-tailed rodent whose feats of backwoods "engineering" are firmly ensconced in American folklore. Using long, ever-growing incisors to chomp down hundreds of aspen and willow trees — his favorite sources of both food and building materials — the beaver probably exerts more influence over his environment than any other animal in the park. His lumberjacking antics regularly open up stream banks to the fresh growth of grasses and wildflowers while his dam-building controls spring floods that would normally scour away aspen and willow saplings.

If you're really serious about seeing a beaver, find a likely looking pond with the characteristic rounded mud-and-stick lodge and then set your alarm for about two hours before sunrise. The beaver is a cerpuscular creature, meaning that he is most active during the low light of pre-dawn and post-dusk. Many people think beavers no longer occupy a pond, when a colony of ten or more adults, yearlings and kits may live there. Rising early and approaching the pond quietly will ensure that you'll be there to catch the action most everyone else misses.

Also, in the Onahu Creek watershed, in fact anywhere in the surrounding Kawuneeche Valley, you may have a chance of spotting the park's newest and largest mammal — the moose. Historically, moose occurred in what was to become Rocky Mountain Park in limited numbers. But the population was so small that they were quickly eliminated by blasts from settlers' rifles. Now, as an offshoot of a wildlife "trade," the moose has returned to Rocky.

In 1977, biologists with the Colorado Division of Wildlife signed an agreement with Utah's Fish and Game Commission. They would receive 12 moose from Utah's Uintah Mountain herd and, in return, provide shipments of blue grouse over a multi-year period. As soon as the deal was confirmed, the Utah moose were transported — using a helicopter and sling arrangement — over several mountain ranges and deposited in historic moose range in North Park, just west of Rocky. The hope was that this basic herd would move into the available habitat and eventually spread to adjacent areas.

So far, the success of this moose transplant has exceeded all expectations. There are now some two hundred moose in Colorado and the population has crossed over the Never Summer Mountains and into the park's Kawuneeche Valley. The best place to look for these massive, often ill-tempered herbivores, is among the head-high willows of the meandering North Fork of the Colorado River.

About three miles up the trail toward Timber Lake, a willow-choked stream meanders through a narrow valley know as Jackstraw Meadows. Here, in icy clear water, lives a population of fish with multi-colored polka dots on their backs and brilliant slashes of crimson along their gills. These are Colorado River cutthroat trout, and their presence represents a significant step forward in the wildlife management of Rocky Mountain National Park.

You're probably familiar with the terms "endangered species" and "extinction," referring to a species of wildlife that has become so limited as to threaten its very existence. When this happens on a localized scale, it's called extirpation, meaning that although the species in question may be thriving elsewhere, it has been locally eliminated from a state or region.

When a species is extirpated, it leaves an unfilled niche or void in the area's wildlife community which presents several problems. It can cause the entire ecosystem to tilt out of balance, just as the absence of wolves and other large carnivores might lead to an overpopulation of deer, elk or moose. Also, an unfilled niche is a beckoning toehold to undesirable exotic or non-native species which can outcompete native species and cause ecological chaos: witness the starling, carp, and Norway rat.

Every extirpated species is still an integral part of Rocky's heritage, a pristine link to "the way it was." This is why the park's staff has been working diligently to restore as many native species as possible. In addition to the Colorado River cutthroat in the Timber Creek drainage, a population of endangered greenback cutthroat trout has been reestablished in the Hidden Valley watershed on the park's east side. Park biologists have, in cooperation with Colorado Division of Wildlife personnel, also released river otters in the Kawuneeche Valley and established several peregrine falcon "hack sites" — artificial nesting areas — on cliffs in the park.

WATER AND ICE. As winter begins to grip the park, look along the streams for scenes such as this. The splashed droplets are frozen in time and the stream will soon lose its battle with the cold.

ASPEN GROVES
& LODGEPOLE STANDS

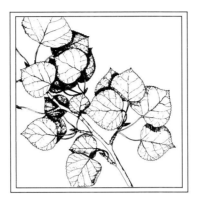

Above 10,000 feet, two pioneer tree species — aspen and lodgepole pine — begin to play a major role in the park's ecology. Fingering down into adjoining forests, both species serve the vital function of revegetating and stabilizing the soil after a forest fire or other major disturbance. But here's where the similarity ends. These two forest types are, quite literally, as different as night and day.

The sun-dappled interior and breezy, refreshing atmosphere make an aspen grove one of the most inviting places in the park to spend a sunny afternoon. Because the delicately-attached leaves tend to tremble and rustle with the slightest breeze, aspen trees are endearingly called "quakies" by native Coloradans.

In contrast, a lodgepole pine forest is generally dark and stuffy. The trees usually grow so close together that they stunt each other's growth, known by natives as "dog-hair stands." The forest floor can be so littered with spindly, fallen timber that it's a chore just to walk. Lodgepoles are names for their flawlessly straight trunks which were perfect for the construction of Indian tepees or lodges.

The contribution these two trees make to a colorful environment is predictably unequal. With a flourish of broad downsweeping strokes, the aspen tree is the brush that paints the park's autumnal landscape. Seemingly overnight, the mountainsides are transformed into a striking mosaic of deep forest greens and cascading yellows, golds and oranges. Meanwhile, with the onset of shorter days, the interior needles of the lodgepole pine turn a dull bronzy-brown and fall silently to the ground.

When it comes to living conditions, lodgepole pines generally take the high road while aspen prefer the low. Typically, lodgepoles grow in broad patches on dry, rocky hillsides while aspen inhabit narrow, well-drained swales.

Although they share a similar role in the ecological process, aspen and lodgepole reproduce in dramatically different ways. If you've ever landscaped with aspen, you know they tend to "sucker out," sending up wild, leafy sprouts all over the place. Typically, all of the trees in an aspen grove share the same root stock. This means that an aspen grove is, in reality, a circular clone of interrelated trees. Because of this, all the trees in an individual grove will turn the same pastel shade in the fall, drop their leaves on virtually the same day and leaf out simultaneously in the spring.

Driving along a twisting mountain highway on a crisp autumn morning, you can easily identify the separate aspen groves. It's not unusual for a clone on one hillside to have lost almost all its leaves while an adjacent clone is just beginning to turn color.

Lodgepole pines, on the other hand, depend on a large assist for successful reproduction. Lodgepole seeds remain sealed inside thick, resinous cones until the heat of a forest fire pops open the scales and

ELK-CHEWED ASPEN TRUNKS. This group of aspen trees show winter forage use by elk. If the elk chew scars completely girdle an aspen trunk, the tree usually dies.

CLUSTER OF COLORADO BLUE COLUMBINES.   The state flower of Colorado graces aspen glades and trailsides in many areas of the park. With colors of its blossom repeating snow-capped peaks and crystal blue skies, the columbine perfectly complements the alpine environment.

WATERFALL AND GOLDEN ASPEN.   This picturesque assemblage of cascading water, shimmering rocks and autumn leaves was discovered near Alberta Falls. It was found just above the spot most people stop to view the falls.

Overleaf: ASPEN PORTRAIT.   Since aspen trees growing this close together probably share a common parentage, subtle differences in soil, moisture availability and other factors must have created this palette of pastel shades.

releases the seeds to the wind.

It follows that if we don't have forest fires, we don't have lodgepole pines. At first thought, that might not seem too bad. But natural, lightning-caused forest fires are vital to a healthy ecosystem. Forest fires are nature's brooms, sweeping away the debris and litter and opening up the forest to the fresh growth of grasses, shrubs and wildflowers. An ecosystem that is allowed to go too long without burning can become too mature, lacking the dynamic growth and vegetative diversity so essential for wildlife.

If you sit for a few minutes and watch an aspen grove, you'll see signs of the many different species that live there. One of the most common sights is the nest hole of the delightfully named yellow-bellied sapsucker. These woodpeckers have distinctive black and white plumage crowned by a red "toupee." They exhibit nesting behavior that would make any equal rights advocate proud. Once the eggs hatch, the male dutifully brings mouthfuls of insects to the squawking chicks. Then, he even takes turns at tending the nursery, allowing the female to stretch her wings on insect-gathering forays. Such "trading places" feeding behavior is exhibited by many bird species and ensures that, should something happen to one of the adults, the nestlings would still have a source of nourishment and parental care.

Another thing you may see is a cup-shaped conglomeration of nesting materials hanging down from a forked elbow of an aspen branch. Closer inspection may reveal the olive-drab head of a warbling vireo perched stoically atop this strange edifice. This wren-sized bird, with its tiny upturned beak and sparkling dark eyes, is one of the best examples of an "indicator species" in Rocky. An indicator species is a plant or animal that is always directly associated with a particular ecosystem. Wherever you go in the Rocky Mountain West, if you happen to see this nondescript bird or hear its languid warble, you can bet there's an aspen grove somewhere nearby.

An aspen grove is also one of the best places in the park for aspiring botanists. The soft sunlight filtering down through delicate foliage provides a perfect, greenhouse-like environment for the lush growth of wildflowers. During a stroll through an aspen grove, you can expect to see scattered stalks of pealike golden banner, boulder-nestled bouquets of Colorado columbine, tiny violet-blue blossoms of harebell, both pink and white geraniums and dazzling pockets of royal purple lupine mixed with fire engine red paintbrush.

While the aspen grove is a beehive of activity, the monoculture of a lodgepole pine stand supports very little life. You might see an occasional showshoe hare scurrying through a patch of purple lupine or hear a chickaree chattering a warning from on high, but chances are they too are just passing through.

Despite all its monotony, the lodgepole forest holds a place of distinction in the park's ecology. Just a scant 80 to 100 years ago, many of the cool, refreshing spruce-fir forests in the park were charred and blackened landscapes. For this amazing transition, we must credit the lodgepole pine.

The lodgepole epitomizes the spirit of the pioneers, those intrepid souls who entered places where others feared to tread and prepared the land for those who would follow. In so doing, they had to bear hardships while the "johnny-come-latelys" reaped all the rewards. This is the lodgepole pine: a struggling pioneer that is a vital link in Rocky's chain of vegetative succession.

EVENING GROSBEAK IN MORAINE PARK. This brightly colored bird uses its oversized bill to crack open seeds. A flock of forty grosbeaks spent more than a month around the Cub Lake Trailhead. When approached they flew to the willow thickets, but soon returned to resume feeding.

SUBALPINE
FOREST

The end result of the successional process started by lodgepole pines is the spruce-fir or subalpine forest. After a forest fire, young lodgepoles take root, sprout and grow, providing the shade needed for the germination of spruce and fir saplings. As the spruce and fir trees mature and grow, they eventually overtop the sheltering lodgepoles and begin to take over the forest. As soon as the last of the· shade intolerant lodgepoles die out, the transition from pioneer pine to climax subalpine forest is complete. Because the frost-free growing season in the high mountains is so short, generally less than three months, this successional process can take more than 100 years.

Subalpine forests are the most common vegetative community in the park between 9,000 and 11,5000 feet. This forest's primary tree species, the subalpine fir and the Engelmann spruce, can be easily identified by a simple rule of thumb: "S" stands for sharp and spruce, while "F" means flat and fir. The needles of the Engelmann spruce are square and quite sharply pointed, so when you squeeze a handful you generally say, "Ouch!" The needles of the subalpine fir, on the other hand, are flat, flexible and quite soft to the touch.

You'll notice that the subalpine forest is generally 10-15 degrees cooler and quite a bit more humid than any of the forests on the slopes below. In the ecological scheme of things, the spruce-fir zone functions like a gigantic snow fence, catching and holding snow that blows off the unprotected tundra. It's not unusual for snow in the subalpine forest to pile up to more than five feet. Sometimes, after a particularly severe winter, this immense snowpack may linger into early fall and blend with the first snowfalls of the coming winter.

Based on this, it's easy to understand why subalpine forests are considered to be nature's reservoirs for the western United States. Most of the water flowing down such mighty rivers as the Colorado and the Platte started out as snowfall trapped amid the park's sturdy boughs of spruce and fir.

The floor of the subalpine forest is covered with a variety of both shrubby and herbaceous or non-woody plants. The most abundant of these is broom huckleberry, a type of blueberry that grows to about 18 inches and is an indicator species for the subalpine forest. Another common ground cover plant, growing in shadowy glens, is the subalpine Jacob's ladder — nature's tiny "stairway to heaven." This delicate plant has tiny, pale-blue flowers and emits a surprising skunk-like odor when its leaves are mashed. During the summer, rivulets of water seeping down between the trunks of spruce and fir give rise to such moisture-loving wildflowers as tall chiming bells, white marsh marigolds and yellow monkey-flowers.

ELK NEAR THE SOURCE OF THE POUDRE RIVER. Because of prevailing weather patterns, the west side of the Continental Divide receives substantially more moisture than the east side, creating vegetation and an environment that attracts grazing animals, such as elk.

After the last vestiges of snowpack have disappeared, often not until mid-July, meadows at this elevation become boggy gardens of floral delights. The saturated, grass-choked soil is the perfect medium for the abundant growth of water-loving wildflowers. Looking like perfectly molded china figurines complete with floppy ears and upturned trunks, the pinkish-purple blossoms of elephantella are every child's favorite. Another eye-catching wet meadow flower is the aptly named shooting-star, whose streaming rose-purple petals and yellow-rimmed head give the appearance of a meteor blasting through space. Also, look for the sheeny yellow dogtooth violet or glacier lily, which pops up from the edges of receding snowbanks, and the low-growing, clover-like rose crown.

Watching the activity in a subalpine glen is like being privy to a real-life melodrama. The first performer to take the stage is the villainous-acting Clark's nutcracker. Squawking like a rusty hinge and swooping about on churning wings, this natty gray, black and white member of the jay family seems determined to harass everything in his path.

Next comes the golden-mantled ground squirrel, often mistaken for a chipmunk by park visitors. Acting like an overbearing landlord on rent collection day, he scurries about sticking his nose into everything until he's finally chased away by the nutcracker.

Suddenly the Colorado chipmunk, seemingly playing the role of the imperiled heroine, dashes wildly onto center stage. Keeping one eye open for potential predators and the other scanning the ground for morsels of food, she skitters back and forth across the forest floor. If you look closely at the chipmunk, you'll notice that her striped cheeks, smaller size and upturned tail readily distinguish her from the golden-mantled ground squirrel.

The second act begins with a flurry as the fluffy-headed gray jay, in the truest tradition of the hero arriving to save the day, floats in on silent wings and alights near the nutcracker. But the nutcracker will not tolerate another bird's encroachment on his territory. He chases the smaller, less aggressive gray jay into the shadowy backstage of the surrounding forest.

Playing the traditional melodramatic role of the innocent bystander, the gray-headed junco slips quietly onto the stage. Haphazardly pecking at seeds on the ground and seemingly oblivious to his surroundings, this rusty-backed member of the finch family suddenly finds himself chased by both the nutcracker and the golden-mantled ground squirrel. Meanwhile, from some distant branch a chickaree, playing the part of a jilted suitor perhaps, scolds incessantly but never shows his face.

One of the most common indicators of the subalpine forest is a tiny olive-gray bird you'll probably never see. More likely you'll hear the ruby-crowned kinglet singing boldly from the top of the tallest spruce tree around.

Your odds are much better of spotting one of the most common ground-dwelling residents of the spruce-fir zone, the snowshoe hare. The primary difference between a hare and its rabbit cousin involves the condition of their young at birth. A rabbit's offspring are born naked, blind and quite dependent, while those of a hare enter the world wide-eyed, fully-furred and ready to bound away at a moment's notice.

The snowshoe hare is named for his oversized feet which enable him to glide across drifts of freshly-fallen snow. He changes his pelage or furry coat from rusty brown in the summer to pure white in the winter, hence his other name — the varying hare.

BACKLIT ELK IN VELVET NEAR POUDRE LAKE.   In mid-summer, bull elk are growing their antlers which will be shed the following spring. Many people think of fall as the prime time for viewing elk, but be sure to look for these magnificent animals during summer in the park's higher elevations.

Overleaf: KAWUNEECHE VALLEY AND GROUND FOG.   On mornings when there is a radical temperature difference between the warm ground and cold air, ground fog occurs. Campers in the Kawuneeche Valley often think they've awakened to a totally overcast, dreary day when the weather is crystal clear and sunny just a few hundred feet above.

PHYLLOTOPSIS NIDULANS GROWING ON DEAD ASPEN LOG.   Mushrooms are the visible fruiting bodies of a group of organisms known as fungi, underground masses of threadlike material that serve as nature's chief decomposers. This view from beneath highlights the intricate patterns and textures found in an unexpected place.

CLARK'S NUTCRACKER IN FLIGHT.   This member of the jay family congregates and hovers in the air over many roadside turnouts, giving park visitors a unique opportunity to closely observe birds in flight.

KRUMMHOLZ
WOODLAND

Near the upper limits of the sub-alpine zone, climatic conditions become so harsh that trees can't grow in the traditional manner. Above 11,000 feet, the relentless high mountain winds function like pruning shears, controlling tree growth patterns as efficiently as a bonsai artist. Because of this, trees tend to grow horizontally and inwardly forming widely scattered clumps of "tree islands," known collectively as the krummholz woodland.

Krummholz is a German word meaning "crooked wood." If you look inside a typical tree island, you'll instantly understand the use of the word. The interior is such a tightly compacted phalanx of gnarled, contorted trunks and interwoven branches that it can easily support the weight of a full-grown man. Although krummholz trees seldom grow more than four feet above the ground, many of them are hundreds of years old.

Occasionally, there is sufficient protection for trees at this elevation to grow vertically, but, even then, they don't look normal. The wind still exerts a strong influence on the trees' growth patterns, shearing off branches on all but the leeward sides. The resulting "flag trees" are unfailingly accurate indicators of the direction of prevailing wind.

A tree that manages to be an exception and often grows normally at this elevation is the limber pine. This five-needled white pine seems to thumb its nose at the brutal weather conditions by growing on the most exposed, windswept ridges in the park. When limber pines finally succumb, they leave bleached, gnarled skeletons standing in ghostly defiance to the harshness of the unyielding horizon.

The krummholz woodland provides valuable summer habitat for two of the park's most common ungulates, mule deer and elk. The ecotonal or "edge effect" resulting from the meeting of the irregularly-shaped tree islands and the open tundra produces a buffet of grazing delights. Also, the dense growing krummholz trees offer a wall of wind resistance, providing welcome refuge from icy gusts.

By walking into the krummholz thickets, the massive elk — some of the bulls weighing nearly a thousand pounds — become invisible to the thousands of people who pass by on twisting Trail Ridge Road. If you take an early morning or late afternoon stroll through the krummholz woodland, you may be astonished by the number of elk you see. Moving very slowly and in a non-threatening manner, you may get close enough to hear their gentle bleating and whoofing communication patterns. If you're really lucky, you may see a cow nursing a spring-born calf or watch a dominance tussle between two regally-antlered bulls.

If you really want a thrill, visit Rocky during the last couple weeks in September — the height of the elk rutting or mating season. One of the most captivating experiences in all of nature is listening to a bull elk's "bugle" echoing across a still, frost-laden evening.

The bugle is a territorial challenge that begins as a sonorous drone, gradually increasing in pitch for 10-15 seconds and then ending with a series of short nasal grunts. After a few minutes, you will be convinced that this — like the cry of the loon and the howl of the wolf — is one of the special sounds of the true wilderness. It has that wondrous capacity to simultaneously chill the spine and instill heart-warming pride in the spirit of the natural world.

KRUMMHOLZ TREES IN LATE AFTERNOON LIGHT. The interior of a krummholz thicket reveals the unusual growth patterns taking place. The north sides of the trees are stripped bare of branches and needles while everything else trails back into a more protected area. It is characteristic for the front branches of a small krummholz thicket to die and form a shield, protecting the rest of the tree mass which is growing horizontally downwind.

LIMBER PINES AT TIMBERLINE.   The bleached skeletons of limber pine bear testimony to the extreme harshness of the environment in which they live. These trees near Trail Ridge Road are particularly dramatic in late afternoon light or just after a storm has passed.

UNUSUAL PATTERN OF LIGHT AND CLOUDS ABOVE TUNDRA.   From Trail Ridge Road the atmosphere is viewed with a different perspective and enables you to see phenomena not usually visible at lower elevations. Although the sun was behind the photographers in this photo, its light was somehow focused by the clouds to a point on the opposite horizon.

Overleaf: ELK HERD IN KRUMMHOLZ THICKET.   The krummholz woodland is the preferred summer habitat for many of the park's elk herd. These stunted tree islands near timberline offer cooler temperatures, shelter from the wind, and a diversity of succulent grazing materials.

ALPINE
TUNDRA

There is a point, as you go up a mountainside, at which the climate becomes too severe even for the growth of the scattered knots of krummholz. This "treeline" in Rocky generally occurs at 11,000 feet, although the actual elevation varies according to local aspect and topography.

At first sighting, the "Land Above the Trees" appears to be a bleak and barren landscape. The impression is of a rolling sea of nothingness at the top of the world. In reality, this alpine tundra is the most intriguing ecosystem in the park. It is a fascinating blend of enigmatic weather conditions and ecological adaptations.

There's a saying in Colorado that in the high mountains there are only two seasons . . . winter and the Fourth of July. Spending a typical summer day in the tundra will help you understand such an exaggeration.

Driving up Trail Ridge Road, you are — from an ecological standpoint — moving about 300 miles to the north for every 1000 feet of elevation you gain. Upon reaching the first tundra turnout, you are in an environment that is the biological and climatic equivalent of north-central Alaska.

Even on the warmest of summer days, you lose as much as five degrees on the Fahrenheit temperature scale for every 1000 feet of elevation you gain.

If it's 80°F in Estes Park at 7500 feet, the air temperature will be around 58°F by the time you reach the 12,000 foot summit of Trail Ridge Road. Subtract a significant chill factor for the wind that is always blowing and the effective air temperature will be in the mid-40s. These geographic and climatic oddities often catch many suntanned, short-sleeved park visitors by surprise.

As you walk along an interpretive trail, the first thing you'll notice is that the tundra is hardly the barren wasteland you first imagined. At the peak of the July growing season, it is an incredibly diverse, splendidly-colored carpet of miniature plants. The show begins with the bold, conspicuous blossoms of the alpine sunflower known as rydbergia.

At the other extreme are the delightful, sky-blue petals of the aptly named alpine forget-me-nots. After finding a cluster of these tiny flowers nestled in the shadows of a sheltering rock, you'll truly treasure their memory forever.

In between, you'll find the profuse, bright yellow alpine avens and the Parry primrose whose blood-red flowers and large leaves usually tower above other tundra plants. The distinctive funnel-shaped blossoms of the purple sky pilot and the curious American bistort, which looks like a miniature snow-

TUNDRA VIEW OF FOREST CANYON AND LONGS PEAK. Late afternoon sunlight creates a pastel mosaic of open tundra, krummholz woodland, subalpine valley and rocky peaks which provides a perfect visual description of Rocky Mountain National Park.

ball mounted atop a tiny flagpole, will also be common sights. You'll be surprised to find there is even a tundra "tree," the snow willow, which grows to a maximum height of four inches.

Just as many park visitors must stop to pull out sweaters and windbreakers as soon as they reach the tundra, tundra plants have made adaptations to cope with this abnormally harsh climate. First and foremost is their consistently small size. Most tundra plants do not grow more than a few inches away from the protective shelter of the ground. Instead, they direct their energy into low, spreading growth patterns, producing mat-like cushion plants. Two of the best examples of this can be seen in the tightly clustered blossoms of the alpine forget-me-nots and the dainty, pink flowers of the moss campion.

Many tundra plants are covered with a mass of soft white hairs known as pubescence. This gives them a distinctive greying appearance and functions like a down coat, holding moisture in and keeping chilly winds out.

Finally, in direct contrast to their limited amount of above-ground foliage, most tundra plants have extensive perennial root systems. This allows them to make maximum use of the limited moisture available in the rock-hard tundra ground.

The tundra receives less effective precipitation than any other ecosystem in the park. The bulk of moisture that falls up here is in the form of snow, most of which blows off into the spruce-fir forest before it has a chance to melt and seep into the frozen ground. Because of this, the tundra is — in effect — a mountaintop desert. Pubescence, cushiony growth forms and far-reaching root systems are three ways tundra plants avoid desiccation or extreme drying out.

Tundra plants are also adept at adhering to the adage "make hay while the sun shines." For instance, the rydbergia always points its large yellow blossoms due east, directly into the path of the rising sun. Walking

through a patch of these "Old Men of the Mountain," with their heads all oriented the same way, it's easy to understand how this composite got another one of its nicknames — The Compass Flower.

At this elevation, the growing season is extremely short. Tundra plants must sprout, grow, bloom, pollinate and go to seed, in six to eight weeks — about half the time it takes for this cycle at lower elevations. This is why, as soon as the high altitude sun has sufficiently warmed the winter-hard ground, the tundra seems to explode in a multi-colored quilt of tiny blossoms. Time is always of the essence in the park's high country and, somehow, tundra plants seem to know it.

The tundra is also home to a cadre of remarkably well-adapted animals, such as Colorado's official state mammal — the Rocky Mountain bighorn sheep. This denizen of the park's high country is at his leisure on the rockiest of precipices and steepest of slopes. Relying on highly specialized hooves, with a soft inner core for traction surrounded by a sharp outer edge, the bighorn can easily go where most other animals fear to tread. These mountaineering wizards spend most of the day on their stratospheric perches, grazing languidly on patches of grass interspersed among the rocks.

The horns of bighorn sheep continue to grow throughout their lives, eventually producing the legendary "full curl" rams so desired by sport hunters. This is in direct contrast to the antlers of deer and elk which sprout, grow, fall off, and then resprout, every year.

A common sight among the numerous rocky outcrops that dot the tundrascape is the park's resident bonvivant — the yellow-bellied marmot. The western equivalent of the eastern woodchuck, this lowslung waddling rodent seems to live the classic "Life of Riley." He spends most of his time lolling in the sun and fattening up on lush summer vegetation.

The marmot is not nearly as relaxed and unaware

TUNDRA VIEW LOOKING TOWARD ROCK CUT. This wide angle view shows the expanse of the tundra plant community. To cope with low temperatures, wind and limited moisture, tundra plants exhibit low, cushiony growth patterns, extensive root systems, and other adaptations which allow them to endure a hostile environment.

WHITETAILED PTARMIGAN ON TUNDRA ROCK. Plumage of the ptarmigan often matches the predominant colors in the surrounding landscape. Here, the white breast and splotches of mottled brown on its back and head indicate the season is early June when the tundra's snowbanks are just beginning to recede.

RYDBERGIA AND MOUNTAINS. This largest of the tundra composite flowers often covers the alpine landscape in a carpet of brilliant yellow, lending contrast to the stark beauty of Forest Canyon and the surrounding peaks. Rydbergia is endearingly known as Old-Man-of-the-Mountains.

Overleaf: YELLOW-BELLIED MARMOTS ON TUNDRA OUTCROP. This view of the high altitude relative of the woodchuck shows its typical high country habitat. Marmots spend most of the day atop boulders, eating, basking in the sun and maintaining a constant vigil for predators.

as he seems, however. Should danger — in the form of a potential predator — approach too closely, he'll quickly rise up and emit a shrill whistle to warn all his compatriots within hearing distance to take cover. He'll then laboriously scurry to the security of his own rock-lined den.

As a true hibernator, the marmot lowers his body temperature and metabolism to near the freezing point, eliminating the need for food intake during the winter months. By contrast, the black bear does not actually hibernate, but instead maintains his body temperature near normal while entering a prolonged period of deep sleep known as dormancy. It's not unusual for a bear to awaken and emerge from his den to feed several times during the winter.

Some of the park's marmots — as well as jays, chipmunks and ground squirrels — have become accustomed to handouts from visitors. Although the idle marmot may look plenty plump and contented, chances are — if he's been eating a lot of peanuts, popcorn, potato chips and other typical offerings — he's really not doing that well. The problem is that while there is always plenty of natural food available during the park's prime visitation months — June through August — it's so much easier for these animals to beg snacks from visitors.

Many of the birds and mammals that frequent parking turnouts may become so dependent on visitor handouts they lose the ability and desire to compete for natural food. As a result, when the weather turns cold and most of the visitors leave, these cute and endearing beggars may starve to death in a world of plenty. So, please do the animals of Rocky a favor and save your food for your own family.

Another of the tundra's most common residents is not likely to be seen. The white-tailed ptarmigan is a master of environmental camouflage, changing from a mottled brown plumage in the summer to pure white in the winter. This plump, grouselike bird's system of cryptic coloration blends so perfectly with the tundra environment, you can walk right past a large flock without even knowing they're there.

During the winter, these incredibly well-adapted birds subsist on the buds of willow branches sticking up through the snow. Their feathered feet allow them to tread nimbly across snowdrifts. To gain additional insulation from subzero temperatures and frigid winds, they dig roost holes in snowbanks and often are completely buried under several inches of freshly-fallen snow.

Several other birds nest on the tundra and can be seen regularly during the summer months. The slender, brown-streaked water pipit is one of the best indicators of the alpine tundra. This sparrow-sized bird always seems to be around, flitting up and down or hopping from rock to rock with a distinctive, tail-bobbing gait.

Perhaps the most unexpected tundra bird is the horned lark which is generally thought of as a resident of Colorado's eastern plains. This ground-loving bird, slightly larger than a sparrow, is named for the black, hornish-looking tufts of feathers on its head.

The task of surviving on the tundra requires all the energy most plants and animals can muster. Any kind of human disturbance, no matter how slight, can be extremely damaging to such a fragile environment.

For this reason, the National Park Service has devised a stringent program to manage and protect the park's tundra. At each tundra parking area, there are meandering asphalt paths designed to let visitors examine this unique resource without trampling it to death.

Few people realize how little effort it takes to severely damage tundra vegetation. If you walk across the grass at home, the next day it will look the same. But up here, those same innocent footsteps can take decades off the life of a tundra plant. Renowned ecologist Beatrice Willard calculated that it takes up to 450 years for a patch of tundra to completely recover from excessive trampling. So let's stay on the trails and save the tundra for the next generations of visitors to see and enjoy.

BIGHORN RAMS IN ALPINE TUNDRA. During summer, bighorn rams congregate in
bachelor herds away from ewes and lambs. They often stay above timberline where their
superbly adapted mountain climbing abilities provide safety among the high peaks.

GLACIATION
& CIRQUE LAKES

While the tundra is the park's most significant biological resource, honors in the physical realm must go to Rocky's glacial geology. Glaciation is responsible for the many marvelously crafted peaks that adorn the tundra's upper echelons. Glaciers formed the square top of Longs Peak by extracting a chunk of terrain from each side of the massive fault block. The Keyboard of the Winds, just east of Longs Peak, was composed when moving masses of ice scooped out both sides of a long ridge. The remaining rock was then fine-tuned to its present configuration by continuous freeze-thaw erosion. Several huge glaciers plucked out massive headwalls to leave the unusual pyramidal pattern of Pagoda Peak.

During the last Ice Age, glaciers moved down mountainsides and into the river valleys below creating many of the park's most distinctive physical features. Like giant ice cream scoops, the moving masses of ice quarried the bases of mountains and carried away the resulting jumble of boulders which were deposited as "erratics" or out-of-place rocks many miles away.

The mountain-shrouded, bowl-shaped cirques that were left soon filled with water and became small lakes called glacial tarns. In some instances, glaciers left whole stairstepping chains of these rock-walled tarns, known as paternoster lakes.

As they moved, glaciers gouged narrow V-shaped river valleys into broad U-shaped valleys. Forest Canyon, traversing the heart of the park, and the ten-mile long Kawuneeche Valley, along the western edge, are two prime examples of glaciated subalpine valleys.

Some of the best examples of the work of a moving glacier can be seen during a hike up to 11,760-foot Chasm Lake. Along the way, you pass high above a magnificent glacially-carved valley and the luminescent, turquoise water of Peacock Pool — a perfect paternoster lake.

Chasm Lake itself is the crown jewel, a fitting reward for the 4.2 mile hike up from the trailhead. With climbers clinging like flies to The Diamond of Longs Peak directly above, Chasm Lake offers one of the most breathtaking panoramas in the park. A host of prominent geologic features such as the Ship's Prow, the Flying Buttresses of Mount Meeker and the Saddle of Mount Lady Washington embellish the familiar outline of Longs Peak. The lakeshore is dotted with large, irregularly-shaped erratics that were plucked from the surrounding rocky façades thousands of years before.

Cirque lakes, such as Chasm, are home to a curious little rodent-like creature that is a close relative of the rabbit. Never failing to announce his presence, the pika uses the magnificent acoustics of his rock-walled amphitheater to issue a resounding "enk-enk." Also known as the alpine haymaker, this round-eared, tawny herbivore doesn't hibernate and so must busy himself cutting and storing grasses and wildflowers beneath the rocks for winter nourishment. Chances are, if you're patient enought to follow his nasal alarm calls and find him amid the lichen-splashed rocks, he'll be dashing hither and yon with a stalk of mid-winter dinner dangling from his mouth.

Popping up like punctuation marks across the tundra, the striking purple-etched, white blossoms of the arctic gentian add an element of floral surprise for late summer visitors to Chasm Lake. These hardy wildflowers, resembling demitasse cups made of the finest china, bloom long after other wildflowers have faded from the landscape. Because of this, they are unfailing harbingers of the coming winter.

BIG THOMPSON AT MOONSET. By consulting a lunar schedule, it's possible to determine exactly when moonset and sunrise occur simultaneously. Here the receding moon is reflected in the river water while the light of the rising sun gives a warm glow to the peaks beyond.

YAWNING PIKA ON TUNDRA.   This five inch long relative of the rabbit is unique to the tundra in that it does not hibernate. Instead, it stores grasses under rocks and ledges and feeds off of them throughout the winter.

TAPESTRY OF ROSY PAINTBRUSH, ELEPHANTELLA, BISTORT AND YELLOW COMPOSITES NEAR POUDRE LAKE.   Wildflowers throughout the park are spectacular at many different times during the summer. By simply changing altitude you can see the same species of flower at various stages of development and adaptation.

Overleaf: CHASM LAKE AND LONGS PEAK AT SUNRISE.   A hike to Chasm Lake by moonlight is as invigorating as it is rewarding. First light of day on the 14,000 foot peak hits with the intensity of a thousand floodlights against the background of a still-dark sky.

KEYBOARD OF THE WINDS.   The precipitous spires of this geological feature, just off the summit of Long's Peak, demonstrate the formidable forces of glacial erosion. The sculpting process is ongoing, as freeze-thaw action continually splits off splinters of rock from the massive headwall.

WATERFALL AND CIRQUE BASIN.   This sunset view of cascading water, flanked by the Keyboard of the Winds, was captured high in this glacier-scoured basin just west of Long's Peak.

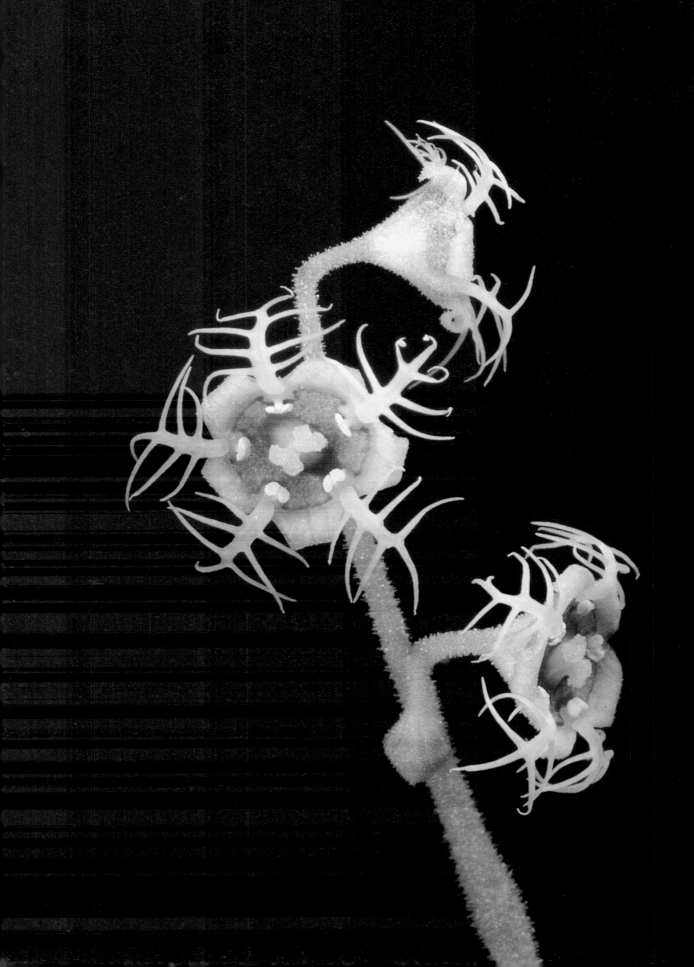

EPILOGUE

Not long ago, I sat with my feet dangling over the edge of a canyon in Dinosaur National Monument, sipping my morning coffee and soaking in the magnificent panorama that was unfolding before me. As the rising sun sent its golden shafts spinning down into the canyon's deepest recesses, I wondered, "Do we really understand and appreciate what we have in a place like this?"

What is the value of our national parks and monuments? Are they vast storehouses of energy reserves . . . an insurance policy for the future? Are they huge recreation centers, places where we can go to "get away from it all" and really let off steam? Are they reservoirs of genetic diversity, preserving as many different species of wildlife as possible? Are they living museums, preserving intact examples of every kind of ecosystem in the United States?

Henry David Thoreau once wrote, "In wildness is the preservation of the world." Thoreau's statement summarizes something that I think we all sense from time to time: There's something in the natural world that we know we can't live without. It's an intangible feeling, very difficult to describe, and yet it's always there in the back of our minds. It's an irresistible urge that makes us all — hikers, campers, sightseers, hunters, fishermen, bird watchers —

yearn to return to nature.

Because of this, we place an intrinsic value on our national parks. Somehow — even if we never get to visit them — just knowing that they're there is quite comforting and satisfying.

What then would we lose if we lost our national parks? Let's examine this question from the standpoint of the grizzly bear. The "Great Bear" once roamed throughout the continental United States, from the plains to the tundra. Now it is confined to remnant populations in· and around Glacier and Yellowstone National Parks.

Enos Mills, naturalist and founder of Rocky Mountain National Park, spent a lifetime tracking and studying the grizzly. He said, "Without the grizzly, there can be no true wilderness." Many members of the ecological community agree with this statement.

Does the disappearance of the grizzly mean that there is no longer any wilderness in most of the "Lower 48" states? Is it possible to have a national park without wilderness? How many wilderness values — such as the grizzly — can we afford to lose before we can say that we have lost a park?

A better question to ask is, how can we best protect the wilderness values we have left? In her book, *The Yearling*, Marjorie Kinnan Rawlings wrote: "We were bred of the earth before we were born of

BISHOP'S CAP. Unseen until revealed by close inspection, the ¼" flower of the bishop's cap is an example of complex creations nature often does in miniature. The delicate plant is found in moist ground often in the company of other inconspicuous flowers such as the bog orchid and heart-leafed twayblade.

Overleaf: LONGS PEAK AND BLOWING SNOW. The compressed perspective of this telephoto view taken along the road to Bear Lake vividly demonstrates the severity of high mountain weather than can occur any day of the year.

our mothers. Born, we can live without our mothers or our fathers but we cannot live without the earth . . . or apart from it. And something is shriveled in man's heart when he turns away from the earth and concerns himself only with the affairs of men."

Rawlings' message is clear: We should strive to live in harmony with the earth instead of constantly struggling for dominance over it. Every potential impact should be looked at like a piece in a gigantic jigsaw puzzle. If the rest of the puzzle has been well thought out, then the new piece will slip easily into place. But if the puzzle has been hastily and sloppily constructed, the new piece won't fit. Forcing it into place will cause the entire puzzle to buckle and break apart.

The same thing happens to the natural environment. Ill-advised, poorly planned development does not fit. It destroys critical natural resources and creates a ripple effect — like a stone tossed into a pond — that sends shock waves throughout the entire ecosystem of interrelated organisms.

How does this apply to our national parks? Let's examine the ultimate questions of park management: Should we manage our parks strictly as wilderness enclaves, minimizing the construction of visitor facilities and transportation routes? This would provide maximum protection for natural resources. But what about those visitors who don't have the time or ability to hike or backpack? How would they see and enjoy the parks?

Should we provide facilities and access points to accommodate every type of visitor? This would ensure that every American would have an equal opportunity to use the parks. But it would also jeopardize the quality of the natural resources the parks are supposed to protect. Which way would you vote . . . in favor of resource protection, or visitor use? If you think this is a tough decision, you're not alone. The National Park Service has been struggling with this dilemma for many years.

The key would seem to be using a balanced approach, weighing the benefits of development against the value of resources that would be lost. If the scale tips in favor of resource preservation, then our plans should be modified accordingly.

This requires continuous communication and co-operation among us all — ecologists, engineers, park managers, concessionaires, visitors. Everyone must be willing to sit together and hammer out compromise plans that will allow needed development to take place in harmony with resource protection. Then we can rest assured that our national parks will forever remain as lasting tributes to the preservation of our national heritage.